Contents

FANTASTIC WORD SEARCH PUZZLES for KIDS

MARK DANNA

PUZZLE WRIGHT PRESS

New York

For my nephews and niece, who have lots of fun
playing with words

PUZZLE
WRIGHT
PRESS
New York

An Imprint of Sterling Publishing
387 Park Avenue South
New York, NY 10016

PUZZLEWRIGHT PRESS and the distinctive Puzzlewright Press logo
are registered trademarks of Sterling Publishing Co., Inc.

© 2004 by Mark Danna

This edition published in 2013.

ISBN 978-1-4549-0971-2

Distributed in Canada by Sterling Publishing
c/o Canadian Manda Group, 165 Dufferin Street
Toronto, Ontario, Canada M6K 3H6
Distributed in the United Kingdom by GMC Distribution Services
Castle Place, 166 High Street, Lewes, East Sussex, England BN7 1XU
Distributed in Australia by Capricorn Link (Australia) Pty. Ltd.
P.O. Box 704, Windsor, NSW 2756, Australia

For information about custom editions, special sales, and premium and
corporate purchases, please contact Sterling Special Sales
at 800-805-5489 or specialsales@sterlingpublishing.com.

Manufactured in the United States of America

2 4 6 8 10 9 7 5 3 1

www.puzzlewright.com

Introduction

The word "fantastic" means many things, including wildly imaginative, ingeniously designed, and based on fantasy. All three of those meanings apply to this book—right from the opening puzzle, which is shaped like a unicorn and filled with the names of fantastic creatures. Word searches in most other books, magazines, and newspapers are fairly ordinary. The puzzles here are truly extraordinary.

What makes these puzzles so fantastic? First, each puzzle grid is a picture. Instead of the usual ho-hum square or rectangle, the grid letters form shapes like a sea horse, a flamingo, a football helmet, an electric guitar, stacked bottles in a carnival game, a Mardi Gras mask, a globe, and a tornado. There are 53 puzzles in all—each one in an exciting shape geared to the puzzle's theme.

To jazz things up, we've added some twists. In four puzzles, it's up to you to build the word list based on our clues. In "Takin' the Rap," you'll need to figure out the rhymes in a rap song. In "Before and After," you'll play a version of a puzzle seen on TV's "Wheel of Fortune." In "Take Note," you'll uncover words that have two meanings. And in "Six of One" you'll add a different letter of the alphabet to the middle of each word.

For more variety, try the rebuses. In these puzzles, little pictures represent a set of letters inside the big picture. For example, in "Sea Here!" every word or phrase in the word list contains the letters SEA in consecutive order. When these letters appear in the sea-horse-shaped grid, they appear as a ⌇ (sea wave). So the phrase FROM SEA TO SHINING SEA in the word list would show up in the grid as FROM⌇TOSHINING⌇. In other rebus puzzles, you'll find little clocks, halt signs, up and down arrows, and numbers.

As a bonus, every puzzle contains a hidden message! After you've circled all the words and phrases in the grid, read all the uncircled letters from left to right, top to bottom, to spell out the answer to a "punny" riddle, a punch line to a silly joke, or words connected to the theme. When you try to uncover the hidden message, the letters will be in order, but you'll need to figure out how to break them into words and where to add punctuation. That makes this puzzle-within-a-puzzle a real challenge and adds a level of difficulty not usually associated with word search puzzles. If you find it too hard, that's okay. You can get still get your laughs by reading the messages in the answer section.

Finding the hidden messages may be tough, but learning to solve word searches is easy. If you know how to do them, you can jump in right now. If you don't know how to do them, keep on reading and we'll tell you everything you need to know.

What's a word search puzzle? A word search is a game of hide-and-seek: we hide the words; you go seek them. Each puzzle has two main parts: a grid and a word list. The grid looks like a meaningless jumble of letters, but it actually hides all the words and phrases in the word list. Most word search grids are square or rectangular, but in this book each grid comes in a distinctive picture shape that relates to the theme of the puzzle.

Words and phrases always go in a straight line—horizontally, vertically, or diagonally. Horizontal words go straight across to the right or backward to the left. Vertical words go straight down or straight up. Diagonal words slant from left-to-right or right-to-left and go either upward or downward along the angle. So words can go in eight possible directions—along the lines of a plus sign (+) or a multiplication sign (×).

What else should I know? In the grid, the same letter may be used in more than one word. This happens when words cross each other from two or more directions. You'll see lots of shared letters in this book because we've made sure that every word in a grid crosses at least one other word, and that all the words in a grid interconnect. It's a nice touch that's often missing elsewhere.

When you look for words and phrases in the grid, ignore all punctuation and spacing in the word list. For example, the phrase

"NOBODY'S HOME!" in the word list would appear in the grid, in some direction, as NOBODYSHOME. Also, ignore all words in brackets like [THE] and [A]. These have been added at times to make certain word list choices more understandable, but they will not appear in the grid.

How do I get started? Some people look for across words first. Others begin with the long words or ones with less common letters like Q, Z, X, or J. Still others start at the top of the list and work their way in order straight down to the bottom. Try a few ways and see what works best for you.

How do I mark the hidden words? Loop them, draw a straight line through them, or circle each individual letter. Whatever you choose, cross the words off the word list as you find them in the grid so as to avoid confusion. And be sure to be neat. Neatness will help when you're looking for all the letters that make up the hidden message.

What's in this book? There are 53 puzzles, each with a different shape and theme. Word lists generally have 20 to 25 items. With a few exceptions, the puzzles are all about the same difficulty level, so feel free to jump around and do the puzzles in any order you like.

Any final words? The puzzle titles are playful, so don't be surprised if you're fooled at first as to what the puzzle theme is. And be prepared for a lot of good, silly fun in the hidden messages. Finally, have a great time from start to finish—from "That's Fantastic!" straight through to "One Last Time."

—Mark Danna

1. THAT'S FANTASTIC!

Shaped like the head of a unicorn, the grid contains fantastic creatures from myth and the movies. The hidden message answers the riddle "What did Dracula's frustrated wife say to her husband?"

```
                                          N
                                       R
                    G              O
             Y  O  O  U        C
          M  E  D  U  S  A     I
          R  E  Z  D  P  S  D  N
       R  M  I  N  O  T  A  U  R  I
    S  V  L  A  L  I  E  N  N  S  A
    E  L  I  C  Y  P  R  A  H  N  A  G  G
    A  R  Y  M  E  R  M  A  I  D  M  G  O  E
    S  C  G  A  B  F  I     P  I  X  I  E  N
    E  T  R  O  L  L  N        S  O     L  P
    R  U  T  O  E  E  A           L  Y
    P  B  W  A  T  I  T
    E  L  V  E  S  N  O  T
    N  N  I  L  M  E  R  G  Y
    T  G  N  O  K  G  N  I  K
```

ALIEN	MERMAID
CYCLOPS	MINOTAUR
DRAGON	OGRE
ELVES	PEGASUS
GENIE	PIXIE
GODZILLA	SEA SERPENT
GREMLIN	[THE] TERMINATOR
HARPY	TROLL
KING KONG	UNICORN
MEDUSA	WOLF MAN

2. BE A GOOD SPORT

Shaped like an inline skate, the grid contains things found in a sporting goods store. The hidden message answers the riddle "Why does the girl listen to pop music when she goes inline skating?"

```
      T  B  S  E
   F  C  N  W  A
   R  O  T  E  E  S
   I  U  O  A  T  K
   S  B  A  T  S  A
   B  T  I  S  B  Y
   E  M  R  O  S  A
   E  C  A  A  S  K  L
   T  R  E  A  D  M  I  L  L
   S  O  S  K  A  T  E  S  E  L
   S  Q  H  P  I  S  D  A  P  E  E  N  K
   Y  U  C  U  E  S  T  I  C  K  E  C  S
      E  S  C        D  O  R  Y  L  F
      T  S  K        O  M  E
A  E  S     R  R  O     C  K  N     A  N  R
W  O  E  S  N  E  A  K  E  R  S  L  T  T  L
E  R  T     B  L  J     A  D  E     S  R  S
```

BATS	MITT
CLEATS	OARS
CROQUET SET	PUCK
CUE STICK	SKATES
DARTS	SKIS
FLY ROD	SNEAKERS
FOOTBALL	SNORKEL
FRISBEE	SWEATS
JERSEY	TEES
KAYAK	TENT
KNEE PADS	TREADMILL
MATS	WET SUIT

3. WHIRLED VIEW

Shaped like a globe, the grid contains places and things found on a globe. The hidden message answers the riddle "What do you call a globe that's well-known to everyone in every country?"

```
                        A
        E   A   E   S       N       S
    W   E   D   Q   M   Y   T   O           I
    A   M   O   U   N   T   A   I   N   S       A
    O   U   A   T   R   R   B   Z   T   L       M
R   D   T   S   I   C   E   U   R   O   P   E   E
C   O   U   N   T   R   I   E   S   F   N   P   R
R   O   A   I   R   S   T   S   E   A   S       I
A   S   C   I   L   E   A   C   I   R   F   A   C
    A   F   E   D   M   A   L   I   E   I       A
    I   S   L   A   N   D   S   I   J   S       S
    A   T   U   N   I   S   I   A           E
O           M   G   S   F               K
S                                   A
    E   D   U   T   I   G   N   O   L
            O   I
            O   L   G   U
    S   R   E   D   R   O   B   S
```

AFRICA	DESERTS	[LINES OF] LONGITUDE
AMAZON	EQUATOR	MALI
AMERICAS	EUROPE	MOUNTAINS
ANTARCTICA	FIJI	NILE
ASIA	GULFS	OCEANS
AUSTRALIA	INDIA	PARIS
BAYS	ISLANDS	ROME
BORDERS	LAKES	SEAS
CITIES	LAOS	TOGO
COUNTRIES	[LINES OF] LATITUDE	TUNISIA

4. UP A TREE

Shaped like a Christmas tree ornament, the grid contains things that may be found on or in a tree. The hidden message answers the riddle "What classes did the tree surgeon take in school?"

```
          H  E  T  O
          O        K
          T  S  E  N
          L  T
          G  A  C  C
       S  Q  U  I  R  R  E  L
    A  H  T  E  T  W  K  B  S  M
    P  M  I  U  I  A  T  E  A  N
 E  P  O  R  A  N  O  E  R  I  T  I
 S  L  S  F  S  I  S  L  R  T  I  S
 R  E  S  E  A  D  S  O  Y  E  N  A
 N  S  O  T  R  E  E  H  O  U  S  E
    D  L  I  N  V  L  T  G  E  E
    O  B  I  M  R  E  O  I  T  L
       V  K  R  A  B  N  R  K
          E  C  E  K
```

APPLES	LEAF
BARK	NEST
BATS	NUTS
BERRY	SNAKE
BIRDS	SQUIRREL
BLOSSOM	TINSEL
CARVED INITIALS	TIRE ON A ROPE
INSECTS	TREE HOUSE
KITE	TWIG
KNOTHOLE	VINES

5. 2, 4, 6, 8

Every item in the word list contains the consecutive letters TWO, FOUR, SIX, or EIGHT. But in the grid, these letters appear as the numbers 2, 4, 6, or 8. So, for example, CLINT EASTWOOD in the word list appears as CLINTEAS2OD in the grid. We hope you appreciate this puzzle. ("2, 4, 6, 8, who do we appreciate?") The hidden message is a sentence with more number-filled words.

```
            4  P  O  S  T  E  R
         A  S  T  2  B  Y  4  S  U  N
      U  N  T  R  U  S  2  R  T  H  Y  O
      2  M  D  A  Y  S  O  4  L  I  V  E  S
      A  N  O  N           A  E  T  D  F
                           R  R  R  E  T
                        W  8  I  A  F  P
            6  E  8  R  F  R  I  A
         R  F  I  T  8  R  2  2  L  E
      4  N  E  8  H  D  O  W  8
      S  H  E  N  S  D  K  W
      O  K  O  R  E
      M  T  R  D  N  A  H  F  O  8  L  S  6
      E  D  O  2  S  A  E  T  N  I  L  C  G
      U  E  C  N  E  P  6  F  O  G  N  O  S
      6  P  E  E  D  N  I  K  A  F  O  4  N
```

AIRFREIGHT	HEIGHTEN
ARTWORK	NETWORKS
CLINT EASTWOOD	OVERWEIGHT
"DAYS OF OUR LIVES"	PETIT FOURS
DEEP-SIX	SIXTH SENSE
DRIFTWOOD	SLEIGHT OF HAND
EIGHTH NOTE	"[SING A] SONG OF SIXPENCE"
FOUR OF A KIND	TWO-BY-FOURS
FOUR-POSTER	UNTRUSTWORTHY
FOURSOME	WEIGHT LIFT

6. POOL PARTY

Shaped like a girl's one-piece bathing suit, the grid contains words associated with being at an outdoor swimming pool. The hidden message answers the riddle "Why did the boy who couldn't swim bring a kitchen sink to the pool party?"

```
H                         E
S                         E
W                         N
I  K                   N  I
M  E  W             S  C  R
M  A  R  C  O  P  O  L  O
I  O  I  W  L  L  T  P  L
N  W  U  A  D  A  S  O  H
G  E  S  T  O  W  E  L  C
   H  P  E  H  D  I  F
   T  A  R  A  F  T  Y
   D  L  W  H  R  U  L
   I  U  I  U  E  S  L
R  V  D  N  E  P  E  E  D
R  E  K  G  K  S  L  B  I
L  S  T  S  N  D  G  K  O
   A  R  L  O  S  G  W
   I  N  O  I  T  O  L
      N  E  M  F  G
            S
```

BELLY FLOP	LOTION
CHLORINE	MARCO POLO
COLD	MOUTHFUL
DEEP END	NOODLE
DIVE	SPLASH
DUNK	SWIMMING
FILTER	TOWEL
GOGGLES	TRUNKS
LANES	WADE
LAPS	WATER WINGS

7. CAN YOU STAND IT?

Shaped like a flamingo standing on one leg, the grid contains things you stand on. The hidden message is a rhyming answer to the question "What do you call an upside-down balancing act performed where a group of musicians play?"

```
        I  T  D  S
     A  E  S  A  B
  B  A        E  N
        L  H
     A  A
     C  N           D  S  T  G  C
  S  D        L  A  D  D  E  R  A  H  N
  S  U  B  W  A  Y  D  Y  N  O  C  L  A  B  H
  A  T  E  R  N  S  K  I  S  U  I  K  N  I  R  B
     Y  M  O  U  N  T  A  I  N  T  O  P  D  R
           S  T  C  T  I  E  D  E  C  K
              P        L
              I           T
              T           S
     M  R  O  F  T  A  L  P
     A              M
                    H
                    T
                    A
              N  D  B
```

BALCONY

BASE

BATH MAT

[THE] BRINK

CHAIR

CURB

DECK

DUTY

GROUND

[YOUR] HANDS

[YOUR] HEAD

LADDER

LINE

MOUNTAINTOP

PLATFORM

SCALE

SKIS

STILTS

SUBWAY

TIPTOE

8. MY I

Shaped like a head and stalk of broccoli, the grid contains words that end in the letter I. The hidden message contains three foods that also end with an I.

```
            S  I  I  Z
            S  H  P  U  Z  I
         C  A  A  I  A  S  Z  C
         M  H  N  F  E  G  I  U
      F  I  J  I  G  E  A  I  H  F  C  C
   T  H  N  K  R  H  N  I  R  C  E  I  A  A
L  A  A  I  H  C  A  B  I  H  I  M  T  C  J  A
M  X  B  M  R  H  I  V  I  T  I  H  A  T  S  M
R  I  I  A  C  I  N  C  I  N  N  A  T  I  I  A
N     P        P  D  M  O  O  S        S     O
      E        P  U  I  L  V  L     S
            P  O  S  A  L  A  M  I
            P  Y  M  O  L  S
            O  E  I  P  S  S
            T  T  R  I  A  U
            A  I  P  O  K  S
            M  P  I  H  N  H
            I  Q  A  R  I  I
```

BIKINI	JACUZZI	SALAMI
CACTI	MAHIMAHI	SCI-FI
CINCINNATI	MIAMI	SHANGHAI
FIJI	MINI	SPAGHETTI
HIBACHI	MISSISSIPPI	SUSHI
HIPPOPOTAMI	PARCHEESI	TAHITI
HOI POLLOI	PEPPERONI	TAXI
IRAQI	RAVIOLI	YETI
	SAFARI	

9. BLOWHARDS

Shaped like a whirling tornado, the grid contains words associated with the wind. The hidden message answers the question "What did the pitcher on the girls' softball team do when it got really breezy?"

```
            E  J  S  T  H
         E  W  Z  E  E  Y  N  P  G
      W  H  T  E  T  I  P  I  L  N  U
   T  O  O  U  E  S  H  H  W  E  R  W  S
   I  S  S  L  R  T  W  O  D  A  N  R  O  T
      N  T  Q  B  R  H  O  D  C  E  L  U  U
         P  O  U  E  I  N  Y  T  W  R  I
            T  R  A  R  C  S  H  B  I  T
               M  L  I  A  U  H  W
               O  W  L  L  N  E  S
            N  T  I  E  U  Y  E
         E  O  W  N  P  L
         L  R  C  D  R
         A  E  R  E
      I  G  A  T
      N  F  S
      T  E  T
      W  D  E
      U  P  R
```

BLOW	STORM
BREEZE	SWIRL
CYCLONE	TORNADO
GALE	TURBULENCE
GUST	TWISTER
HOWL	TYPHOON
HURRICANE	UPDRAFT
JET STREAM	WESTERLY
NOR'EASTER	WHIP
SQUALL	WHIRLWIND

10. TEAM PLAYERS

Shaped like a football helmet, the grid contains the team name for a player on each of the 32 teams in the National Football League. Twenty-six of those team players appear in the word list and should be circled in the grid as usual. The remaining six can be found in alphabetical order in the hidden message.

```
            B  C  O  W  B  O  Y
         R  L  L  O  C  N  O  R  B  E
      F  N  A  L  N  I  H  P  L  O  D  K
      R  E  N  I  N  Y  T  R  O  F  W  B  G
   A  L  O  I  B  D  E  E  L  G  A  E  N  C
   B  I  O  D  H  L  E  V  C  H  A  R  G  E  R
   L  U  T  R  N  C  F  R  A  R  A
   L  G  C  A        C  E  O  R
   N  N  T  C        S  K  N
   J  I  G  I  A  N  T  C  A
   T  K  K  G  U  N  E  A
      I  A  S  I  A  E  P  A  T  R  I  O  T  R
      V  J  A  D  X  L  E  E              T
         S  R  A  E  E     R  E  H  T  N  A  P
            M  T  R
```

BEAR	DOLPHIN	RAIDER
BILL	EAGLE	RAVEN
BRONCO	FORTY-NINER	REDSKIN
BROWN	GIANT	SAINT
BUCCANEER	LION	SEAHAWK
CARDINAL	PACKER	STEELER
CHARGER	PANTHER	TEXAN
CHIEF	PATRIOT	TITAN
COWBOY		VIKING

11. PLAY GROUND

Shaped like home plate in baseball, the grid contains things you might find on the ground—in the city, the country, or elsewhere. The hidden message is one more playful thing that would fit nicely on this list.

```
S  K  C  A  R  T  D  A  O  R  L  I  A  R  H
N  T  E  K  N  A  L  B  H  C  A  E  B  A  A
O  R  E  V  O  C  E  L  O  H  N  A  M  G  Y
W  P  S  N  A  K  E  B  E  R  S  M  R  O  B
S  E  V  A  E  L  N  M  U  T  U  A  E  N  A
D  I  R  T  L  E  V  A  R  G  S  W  T  H  L
O  S  D  M  A  D  W  K  F  S  S  I  T  N  E
S  D  E  E  W  P  L  O  S  T  C  O  I  N  S
   Q  G  A  W  L  D  S  R  N  O  R  L  E
      U  E  T  A  L  P  E  M  O  H  L
         I  W  Y  L  W  A  C  S  D
            R  E  N  K  K  G  D
               R  E  S  S  U
                  E  L  P
                     L
```

AUTUMN LEAVES	HOME PLATE	SNAKE
BEACH BLANKET	LITTER	SNOW
BUGS	LOST COINS	SQUIRREL
DIRT	MANHOLE COVER	TACKLED PLAYER
GRASS	PUDDLES	WAD OF GUM
GRAVEL	RAILROAD TRACKS	WEEDS
HAY BALES	ROCKS	WORMS
	SIDEWALKS	

12. TAKE NOTE

Shaped like a musical note, the grid contains words like NOTE that can be defined in more than one way. To find out what those words are, use the clues on the opposite page. Each clue gives two definitions for each word, and the blanks tell you the number of letters in each word. As an extra hint, the missing words from 1 through 19 are in alphabetical order. After you've filled in the blanks, circle the words as usual in the grid. If you need help with the words, the complete list can be found on page 65. As for the hidden message ... well ... it's hidden. In fact, instead of finding it here, you'll find it quite appropriately in "The Sound of Music" puzzle on page 22.

```
                        S
                        E   E
                        S       T
                        S           O
                        E               N
                        R               O
                        D               R
                        I               I
                        A
            B   L   U   E   M
        S   S   O   L   L   A   O
    S   E   E   P   W   T   E   N
    B   V   P   C   C   S   L   D
    U   A   A   H   P   A   G   E
    C   E   T   E   K   C   A   R
        L   E   S   O   R   E
            S   T   A   R
```

CLUES

1. A red fruit, or a computer company that makes iPods _ _ _ _ _

2. What you hit baseballs with, or flying mammals that often hang upside-down _ _ _ _

3. The color of clear skies, or what you are if you're sad _ _ _ _

4. Fancy decorations on presents, or things you use to shoot arrows _ _ _ _

5. Where a king and queen may live, or another name for a rook in chess _ _ _ _ _ _

6. The part of the body where your heart is, or a container for pirates' buried treasure _ _ _ _ _

7. Baby bears, or a Chicago baseball team _ _ _ _

8. The shape of a baseball infield, or a precious jewel in an engagement ring _ _ _ _ _ _ _

9. Clothes that women wear, or puts on clothes _ _ _ _ _ _ _

10. "Bald" bird that is a symbol of the United States, or a Philadelphia football player _ _ _ _ _

11. A golf club that's not a wood, or something you use to remove wrinkles from clothes _ _ _ _

12. Goes away, or things that fall in the fall _ _ _ _ _ _

13. Something you use to light a fire, or a tennis competition _ _ _ _ _

14. Things you take in class, or markings on sheet music _ _ _ _ _

15. A part of a book, or a youth who serves a knight _ _ _ _

16. Noisy shouting, or what you hit a tennis ball with _ _ _ _ _ _

17. A pretty flower, or got up from a chair _ _ _ _

18. A movie celebrity, or part of a constellation _ _ _ _

19. Uses a camcorder, or "finishing" ribbons stretched out at the ends of footraces _ _ _ _ _

13. THE SOUND OF MUSIC

Shaped like an electric guitar, the grid contains places, activities, and things in, at, or on which you hear music being played. The hidden message answers the riddle "What did the girl do with her sheet music from band practice?"

```
                    F C
                  S I E H
                    N L
                  M A L L
                    L P
                    J H
                    E O
    E               O N
    P               P E       U
    T I             A M       T
    E I   C R       A   M N
    H C   O D   G P U E
    R L   N Y   O A S
      E   C A   E R I
      S   E N   D A C O
    T U   R I   I D A E
    R O   T A   V E L E
    B R   O S   T O R E
    P A   R T   Y O M K
      C   H U   R C H
```

CAROUSEL	MALL
CELL PHONE	MOVIE
CHURCH	MUSICAL
CONCERT	PARADE
DANCE	PARTY
ELEVATOR	STORE
FINAL JEOPARDY!	VIDEO GAME

14. WINGING IT

Shaped like an angel in profile, the grid contains things with wings. The hidden message completes this question: "Would you rather be bitten by horseflies or by Pegasus ..."

```
        S  T  A  B
              N
              G
        A  L  E
     K  R  A  L
        H  D  S
           Y        D  M  V
     O  E  B  E  R  R  U  S  F
     S  S  U  A  K  L  S  N  L  E
     T  U  G  W  T  R  E  D  I  L  G
     I  O  R  U  R  N  U  T  E  B  H
     N  H  R  A  A  E  M  T  S  T  O  H
     K  E  S  L  C  O  N  D  O  R  S  R  A
     E  T  P  E     I     M     T     F
     R  I  A  T
     B  H  R  O
     E  W  R  H
     L  L  O  I
     L  E  W  S
```

ANGELS	LARK
BATS	MOTH
BIPLANE	MUSEUM
CONDORS	ROBIN
DRAGON	SPARROW
FLIES	TINKERBELL
GLIDER	TURKEY
HOTEL	VULTURE
ICARUS	[THE] WHITE HOUSE
LADYBUG	WREN

15. IT'S ONLY MONEY

Shaped like a dollar sign, the grid contains words and images that are printed on various denominations of United States currency. The hidden message completes the joke that begins "Did you hear about the girl who was saving for a rainy day?"

```
                U S
                N O
        W A S H I N G T O N O
      N L A E S T A E R G S H
      T I E T L E M L B E A B
      O B N     D U
      R E L     S N
      C R E     T U
      H T T R E A S U R Y E
      T Y O O A T U S T A R S
        F N F D E B T S C O E
            S I     I R Y
            D R     R D E
            A U     E N U
      C A P I T O L M N M B R
      D I M A R Y P N G A L F
      E E S U O H E T I H W
            K L
            L A
```

AMERICA	LIBERTY
CAPITOL	NOTE
CENTS	PYRAMID
DEBTS	STARS
E PLURIBUS UNUM	TORCH
EYES	TREASURY
FLAG	UNITED STATES
[THE] GREAT SEAL	WASHINGTON
KENNEDY	[THE] WHITE HOUSE

16. IN A FIX

Shaped like a pump at a gas station, the grid contains things a car might have problems with—and why it might be brought into a gas station. The hidden message is a sign that a gas station owner with a sense of humor might put up next to his pumps.

```
W  E  X  H  A  U  S  T
G  N  I  L  T  T  A  R
E              A  A
G              N     E
E              S  I     G
N  R  E  L  F  F  U  M  T     V
I  E  G  R  S  E  S  I     N  A
G  N  I  R  E  E  T  S        E
N  E  T  N  R  O  H  S           D
E  Z  S  I  I  E  M  I           I
P  E  T  D  F  O  L  O           S
A  E  A  F  K  S  S  N           C
I  R  E  E  C  A  R  R           S
N  F  B  R  A  K  E  S        H
T  I  U  H  B  V  P  L     I
J  T  R  E  T  L  I  F  M
O  N  I  A  L  C  W  M
B  A  T  T  E  R  Y  E
```

ANTIFREEZE	FILTER	RADIO
BACKFIRES	FUEL	RATTLING
BATTERY	GEARS	SHIMMY
BRAKES	HEAT	SMOKE
DENTS	HORN	STEERING
DISCS	LEAK	TIRES
ENGINE	MUFFLER	TRANSMISSION
EXHAUST	PAINT JOB	WIPERS

17. AW, CHUTE!

Shaped like a parachute, the grid contains words associated with skydiving. The hidden message is a new, funny ending for the old saying that begins "If at first you don't succeed ..."

```
                M  E  D  G  O
             N  E  T  T  N  H  L  T  N
          E  D  U  T  I  T  L  A  I  A  T
       A  N  H  K  D  J  U  M  P  R  E  O  U
    P  A  C  A  N  O  P  Y  S  P  E  N  A  L  P
    T  A  R  A  P  O  O  L  L  A  F  E  E  R  F
    S  O  L  O        A  R  C        H  U  S  T
    I                    I                    S
       S                 P                 T
          K              C              A
             Y           O           T
                D        R        I
                   I     D     C
                      V  N  L
                         I
                      N  W  N
                   E  N     G  G
```

ALTITUDE	PLANE
CANOPY	PULL
CHUTE	RIPCORD
FLOAT	SKYDIVING
FREEFALL	SOLO
HARNESS	SPIN
JUMP	STATIC LINE
LANDING	TANDEM
LOOP	WIND

18. OFF WITH HER HEAD!

In "Alice in Wonderland," the Queen of Hearts commanded, "Off with her head!" So we took the queen to heart and cut off the word HEAD in every word or phrase in the head-shaped grid. For example, the word HEADQUARTERS in the list will appear only as QUARTERS in the grid. Don't let it go to your HEAD, but the hidden message will tell you four more words that can end with HEAD.

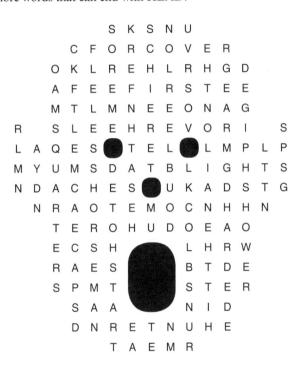

			BLOCKHEAD			HEADHUNTER			HEADSPACE

BLOCKHEAD
COME TO A HEAD
DOUBLEHEADER
HARDHEADED
HEADACHES
HEADDRESS
HEADFIRST
HEAD FOR COVER
HEADGEAR

HEADHUNTER
HEADLESS HORSEMAN
HEADLIGHTS
HEAD LINESMAN
HEADMASTER
HEAD OF LETTUCE
HEAD OVER HEELS
HEADQUARTERS
HEADROOM
HEADS OR TAILS

HEADSPACE
HEADSTART
HEADSTRONG
HIT THE NAIL ON THE HEAD
HOTHEADED
MEATHEAD
PIGHEADED
SHOWERHEAD
SOREHEAD

19. JUMP FOR JOY

Shaped like a hopscotch board, the grid contains things you jump or jump over. The hidden message answers the riddle "Why do you need to calm down when you play checkers?"

```
            P  L  R
         A  Y  E  R  W
         I  K  A  E  A
         C  B  C  Y  L
   N  S  E  H  G  A  A  L  O  G  A
   D  H  G  O  E  N  L  R  N  G  A
   C  I  M  P  P  D  P  U  C  M  E
   H  P  T  S  O  L  G  T  A  C  A
            C  R  E  O  E
            O  H  S  R  N
            T  E  T  F  N
            C  S  I  P  I
   N  M  N  H  A  C  A  S  K  E  Y
   O  E  U  S  H  K  E  N  F  E  R
   F  E  P  Q  U  L  L  E  K  A  I
   N  D  T  U  R  N  S  T  I  L  E
            A  D  O  F  L
            R  L  D  I  J
            E  E  N  L  U
            M  G  P  Y  E
```

A LOG	LEAPFROG PLAYER
CANDLESTICK	PUDDLE
CHECKER	RAILING
CRACK	ROPE
DITCH	SHIP
FENCE	STREAM
HEDGE	TENNIS NET
HIGH BAR	THE GUN
HOPSCOTCH SQUARE	TURNSTILE
HURDLE	WALL

20. A TALL TALE

Shaped like a giraffe, the grid contains things that are or may be tall. The hidden message answers the riddle "Which Major League Baseball team is the tallest?"

```
            I       H
            T       T
      T  S  P  L    A
   S  A  T  H  E    I
   M          F     L
               L    O
               A    G
               G    O
               P    D
               O    Z
            G  L  I  L  I  A  S  T
            R  E  L  E  P  H  A  N  T
            E  A  L  N  I  L  T  R  E  X
            W  T  A  P  E  R  E  E  S  N
            O     D     E     P        I
            T     D     Y     A        H
            L     E     A     R        P
            E     R     L     C        S
            F     E     P     S
            F     D     A     Y
            I     R     B     K
            E     O     N     S
```

ALPS	LADDER	SKYSCRAPER
EIFFEL TOWER	MAST	SPHINX
ELEPHANT	N.B.A. PLAYER	TALE
FLAGPOLE	ORDER	TREE
GODZILLA	SHIP	T. REX
GOLIATH		WALL

29

21. THAT'S NEWS TO ME!

Shaped like a TV with a cable box on top, the grid contains people and things you might hear about on the evening news. The hidden message is a comment about the news that begins "The things that happened today are pretty much the same as yesterday ..."

```
            S  M  R  O  F  E  R
            E  O  X  C  M  E  P
      R  T  H  T  H  V  D  I  L  A  D  N  A  C  S
      O  A  E  S  E  I  T  I  R  B  E  L  E  C  T
      T  T  R  T  H  E  U  C  S  E  R  K  E  Y  S
      A  N  O  I  S  S  I  M  E  C  A  P  S  H  E
      N  A  E  P  E  F  P  L  R  U  O  T  E  N  T
      E  E  M  D  F  C  E  D  Q  O  Y  V  T  S  O
      S  T  I  A  I  C  O  H  O  L  T  D  E  T  R
      I  F  R  F  T  C  T  N  E  D  I  S  E  R  P
      E  T  C  I  R  R  C  S  O  R  E  N  T  O  Y
      G  L  O  B  A  L  W  A  R  M  I  N  G  P  P
      E  N  O  E  F  L  O  O  D  P  Y  F  L  S  E
```

ACCIDENT	FLOOD	SENATOR
CELEBRITIES	GLOBAL WARMING	SPACE MISSION
CRIME	HERO	SPORTS
DISCOVERY	MOVIES	STORM
EARTHQUAKE	PRESIDENT	STYLES
ECONOMY	PROTESTS	TIME
ELECTION	REFORMS	TRAFFIC
FIRE	RESCUE	TRIAL
	SCANDAL	

22. HOT STUFF

Shaped like a sombrero hat, the grid contains foods found in a Mexican restaurant. The hidden message is a punny weather report that could appear on a Mexican Food Channel.

```
            I  T
         L  L  L  E
         B  E  E  N
      T  T  C  C  C  C
      S  O  P  E  H  H
      A  R  S  I  I  E
      L  T  L  T  L  I
L  H  U  E  V  O  S  I  I  I  A  G  O  R  D  I  T  A
T  O  O  N  E  P  A  L  A  J  D  D  I  B  E  A  N  S
D  N  A  L  F  A  E  L  O  M  A  C  A  U  G  Y  A  N
   C  H  A  L  U  P  A  D  H  E  F  O  R  T  T  A
      A                             R
      U                             I
      T                             T
      A  M                       A  O
         A  L              C  E
         N  A  C  H  O  S
```

BEANS	HUEVOS
BURRITO	JALAPENO
CHALUPA	LECHE
CHILI	NACHOS
ENCHILADA	RICE
FAJITA	SALSA
FLAN	SOPE
FLAUTA	TACO
GORDITA	TORTILLA
GUACAMOLE	TOSTADA

23. BEFORE AND AFTER

The TV game show "Wheel of Fortune" often features a category called "Before and After." In this category, a word or words in the middle of the puzzle finish one common phrase while starting another. For example, the phrases "You deserve all the credit" and "credit card" would appear in their puzzle as "You deserve all the credit card."

In this word search, we've changed the game a bit. Instead of guessing the combined phrase, you need to figure out what the word in the middle is. So if we took the example above, it would appear in our puzzle as YOU DESERVE ALL THE _ _ _ _ _ _ CARD. The missing middle word would be CREDIT.

```
                  P  W
                  E  A
               A  S  S  R
         E  T  L  C  H  T  T  A
      D  H  L  H  I  I  F  N  Y  E
      E  I  O  B  E  N  D  A  N  L
   R  B  O  A  M  A  G  I  C  I  C  G
   L  L  A  S  M  S  T  O  F  A  R  O
   L  L  A  B  T  O  O  F  R  T  I  Y
I  N  D  E  P  E  N  D  E  N  C  E
      D  S  A  N  V  E  D  G  U  E
      T  N  J  U  E  T  P  O  O  H
         L  I  B  R  A  R  Y  F
            L  Y  L  I
               B  O
               O  C
               D  O
               Y  H
      C  Y  E  K  C  O  H  E
```

Twenty "Before and After" phrases appear below. Fill in each missing middle word and then find it in the grid. The number of blanks will tell you the number of letters in each word. As an extra hint, the missing words are in alphabetical order. If you can't figure out what goes in some blanks, search for hidden words in the grid that might fit the blanks where you're having difficulty. If you're still stuck, you can turn to the full word list on page 65.

The grid, by the way, is shaped like a wheel of fortune game that stands upright at carnivals and in casinos. The hidden message is one more combined "Before and After" phrase.

CLUES

1. DOLLAR _ _ _ _ COLLECTOR
2. VENETIAN _ _ _ _ _ DATE
3. MILK _ _ _ _ _ _ _ _ CHIP COOKIES
4. ARCTIC _ _ _ _ _ _ OF LIFE
5. BASEBALL _ _ _ _ _ _ _ RING
6. WHERE IS _ _ _ _ _ _ _ _ _ INTO THE POOL
7. TOOTH _ _ _ _ _ GODMOTHER
8. TOUCH _ _ _ _ _ _ _ _ HELMET
9. WATER _ _ _ _ _ _ _ _ PEN
10. ICE _ _ _ _ _ _ STICK
11. HULA _ _ _ _ EARRINGS
12. DECLARATION OF _ _ _ _ _ _ _ _ _ _ _ _ DAY
13. LENDING _ _ _ _ _ _ _ BOOK
14. BLACK _ _ _ _ _ CARPET
15. REPUBLICAN _ _ _ _ _ FAVOR
16. ELEMENTARY _ _ _ _ _ _ BUS
17. DINING ROOM _ _ _ _ _ OF CONTENTS
18. TASTE _ _ _ _ PILOT
19. SEATTLE _ _ _ _ _ _ _ _ _ D.C.
20. STORMY _ _ _ _ _ _ _ FORECAST

24. CLEAN UP YOUR ACT

Shaped like a washing machine with a box of detergent on top, the grid contains things you clean with. The hidden message answers the riddle "Why did the bank robbers use soap and water during the holdup?"

```
        T  D  H
        H  U  E
        S  S  H
        C  T  I
  V  Y  O  R  W  L  H  M  A  P  M
  A  L  U  A  N  T  O  O  E  A  O
  C  D  R  G  Q  T  I  P  S  P  O
  U  D  I  S  H  W  A  S  H  E  R
  U  E  N  T  O  M  A  K  A  R  B
  M  T  G  E           A  M  T  C
  C  E  P              P  O  E
  L  R  A              O  W  E
  E  G  D  R           L  O  E  G
  A  E  E  E  A  S  F  N  G  L  E
  N  N  E  T  O  T  A  L  W  A  E
  E  T  S  A  P  H  T  O  O  T  U
  R  Y  P  W  E  G  N  O  P  S  Q
  C  O  T  T  O  N  B  A  L  L  S
```

BROOM	POLISH
CLOTH	Q-TIPS
COTTON BALLS	SCOURING PAD
DETERGENT	SHAMPOO
DISHWASHER	SOAP
DUST RAGS	SPONGE
FLOSS	SQUEEGEE
HOSE	TOOTHPASTE
MOPS	VACUUM CLEANER
PAPER TOWEL	WATER

25. FOWL PLAY

Shaped like a Christmas tree, the grid contains words and phrases from the popular holiday song "The Twelve Days of Christmas." The hidden message completes this thought: "Except for the fifth day of Christmas, the first seven days weren't so hot. In fact, when you think about it, you could say ..."

```
                        R
                    T   H   A
                G   E   E   S   E
            S   E   I   D   A   L   P
        E   P   Y   I   W   S   Y   A   D
            A   E   D   R   E
            M   S   R   E   P   I   P
        E   M   O   T   T   R   E   E   F
    G   O   L   D   E   N   R   I   N   G   S
C   A   L   L   I   N   G   B   I   R   D   S   O
        G   N   I   C   N   A   D
        L   R   S   W   A   N   S   T   G
    O   D   R   U   M   M   E   R   S   H   E
V   E   B   F   R   E   N   C   H   H   E   N   S
E   U   R   T   U   R   T   L   E   D   O   V   E   S   I
                        R
                        D
                        S
```

CALLING BIRDS	MAIDS
DANCING	PARTRIDGE
DAYS	PEAR
DRUMMERS	PIPERS
FRENCH HENS	SENT
GEESE	SWANS
GOLDEN RINGS	TO ME
LADIES	TREE
LORDS	TRUE
LOVE	TURTLE DOVES

26. HOW SWEET IT IS

Shaped like a honey-bear-shaped bottle of honey, the grid contains things that are sweet. The hidden message completes the joke "The diet doctor told me I can't have ice cream for dessert anymore ..."

```
            S
            R
        O R E O S
        S S K I O
      R E K C U S P
    N I R I A L C E O
    P Y N T R S M A J
      G F O C E A C
      W I F L L P H
        L F A T L
      A C E M T E H
    N A O E I I S V T
    J E T I N R Y A U
    U N T W A B R C N
    J T O A S T U U O
    U R N U S U P S D
    B C C A G N G T N
    E B A K L A V A A
    S G N K P E T R R
      P D E E P T D
      I Y U Z S E R
      P A R F A I T
```

ANIMAL CRACKERS	FLAN	PEACH
BAKLAVA	FUDGE	PEANUT BRITTLE
BROWNIE	ICING	PIES
CAKES	JAMS	SUCKER
COTTON CANDY	JUJUBES	SUGAR
CUSTARD	MAPLE SYRUP	TAFFY
DONUT	NOUGAT	TART
ECLAIR	OREOS	TOFFEE
	PARFAIT	

27. TAKE A BREAK

Shaped like a heart, the grid contains things you break. The hidden message answers the riddle "Why did the bully punch the pleading boy hard in the nose?"

```
      B  W  E              C  N  A
   P  U  I  S  E        W  A  H  E  E
R  R  E  S  A  C  R     E  I  I  S  K  W  A
E  O  I  H  G  D  U     L  W  C  N  I  K  S
T  M  S  B  C  G  L     T  O  A  H  D  O  M
S  I  C  O  N  C  E  N  T  R  A  T  I  O  N
I  S  D  N  I  E  S  W  I  L  S  O  T  O  W
L  E  H  E  N  L  A  G  R  D  P  O  R  I  S
B  S  N  O  O  L  L  A  B  R  E  T  A  W  V
   A  K  A  E  R  T  S  T  E  L  C  E  E
      D  H  I  L  M  S  U  C  L  A  H
         T  H  T  E  A  E  N  O  T  M  A
            I  A  F  B  C  A  R  R  P
               R  B  E  U  E  D  A
                  I  I  R  P  S
                     P  T  K
                        S
```

A TIE	[A] NAIL	[SOMEONE'S] SPIRIT
[A] BAD HABIT	[THE] NEWS	[A] STREAK
[A] BLISTER	PEANUT BRITTLE	[A] SWEAT
CAMP	[A] PROMISE	THE LAW
[THE] CASE	RANK	[A] TOOTH
[THE] CODE	[THE] RULES	[A] TRUCE
[YOUR] CONCENTRATION	SHOELACES	WATER BALLOONS
EGGS	[THE] SKIN	[A] WINDOW
[A] FAST	[THE] SOIL	[A] WISHBONE
[SOMEONE'S] HEART	[A] SPELL	[THE] WORLD RECORD

28. TOOLING ALONG

Shaped like a handsaw propped up on its handle, the grid contains different kinds of tools. The hidden message completes the old joke "'It's a miracle!' said the blind man, as he ..."

```
                    F  I  L  E
                    R  L  A
                 H  I  E  T  E
                 R  V  S  H
              D  L  E  I  E  D
              R  R  T  H  S
              E  E  E  C  O  E
           P  M  T  R  U  L
           L  M  T  S  H  D  P
           I  A  U  A  A  E
        H  E  H  C  N  E  R  W
        A  R  K  E  D  M  I
        M  S  C  R  E  W  N  E
     R  A  A  N  I  R  D  G
  W  U     A  W  L  S  I  S
     G              R  A
     E              O
  T  R  O  W  E  L  W  N
  L  S  R  E  C  N  I  P
  O                 A
  B                 N
```

AUGER	PINCERS
AWLS	PLIERS
BOLT	RIVETER
CHISEL	SANDER
DRILL	SCREW
FILE	SOLDERING IRON
HACKSAW	TROWEL
HAMMER	VISE
LATHE	WIRE CUTTER
NAIL	WRENCH

29. HURRY UP AND GET DOWN TO BUSINESS

Every item in the word list contains the letters UP or DOWN in consecutive order. When these letters appear in the up-and-down-arrow grid, every UP has been replaced by ↑ and every DOWN by ↓. For example, the UPSIDE-DOWN will appear as ↑SIDE↓. So pick ↑ your pencil and get ↓ to it. The hidden message is what an angry grown↑ might say when dressing ↓ a misbehaving child.

				ACT UP		ERUPT		UPFRONT	

ACT UP   ERUPT   UPFRONT
BUCKLE UP   GANG UP ON   UPROAR
DOWN-AND-OUT   RUBDOWN   UPSET
DOWNLOAD   SUNDOWN   UPSIDE-DOWN
DOWNPOUR   SUPERMAN   UPTIGHT
DOWN-TO-EARTH   TOUCHDOWN   UP TO NO GOOD
DOWNTOWN   UP AND AT 'EM   UPWIND
DOWNWARD   UPDATE   "WHAT'S UP, DOC?"

30. ROLL CALL

Shaped like a shopping cart, the grid contains things that roll or are rolled. The hidden message answers the riddle "Why did the good-looking, hard-working girls want to star in a Rollerblade commercial?"

```
T  L  P
   B  U  G  G  Y  R  E  P  A  P  S  W  E  N
      Y  L  G  H  P  H  E  L  Y  T  W  A  A  N
         L  T  G  L  E  D  L  E  T  O  G  B
         T  L  U  A  T  R  A  C  F  L  O  G
         O  E  O  Y  G  M  B  C  O  I  N  S
         Y  R  D  D  R  E  D  N  U  H  T
         D  R  A  O  B  E  T  A  K  S  E
            O  L  H  G  U  R  N  E  Y  L
            L  A  W  N  M  O  W  E  R
      E
   R  L  V  T  U  M  B  L  E  W  E  E  D
         A  M                 O  C
         D  N  W  E           E  R  I  T
         K  L                 S  D
```

BALL	NEWSPAPER
BUGGY	PLAY-DOH
COINS	PULL TOY
DICE	SKATEBOARD
DOLLY	STEAMROLLER
DOUGH	TANK
[YOUR] EYES	THUNDER
GOLF CART	TIRE
GURNEY	TUMBLEWEED
LAWN MOWER	WAGON
LUGGAGE	WAVE

31. STRIP SEARCH

Shaped like a speech balloon, the grid contains the names of characters from syndicated newspaper comic strips. The hidden message answers this quiz: "What title characters of two popular comic strips—a cat and a duck—have the same names as two former presidents of the United States?"

```
        E  I  D  N  O  L  B
     I  G  Z  N  A  N  R  O  F
  D  D  I  F  O  D  R  A  Z  I  W
O  O  G  I  E  S  I  T  R  U  C  S  E
L  G  A  H  T  R  O  F  Y  L  L  A  S
Y  B  H  N  D  E  M  O  O  S  E  H  O
A  E  N  A  I  T  K  D  N  M  E  A  R
L  R  L  M  G  T  C  O  A  A  O  Y  R
   T  D  R  F  A  O  I  T  L  H  L
      M  E  O  P  R  H  R  T  S
         H  Y  Y  C  N  A  N
            L  O  C
            I  L  E
         F  R  E
      F  A
```

ARLO	HAGAR	ROSE
BLONDIE	HEATHCLIFF	SALLY FORTH
CATHY	HERMAN	SHOE
CROCK	LOIS	SNOOPY
CURTIS	LUANN	TINA
DOGBERT	MOOSE	[THE] WIZARD OF ID
ELLY PATTERSON	NANCY	ZIGGY
	ODIE	

32. GOING PLACES

Shaped like a home, the grid contains places you might go to during the course of a typical day. The hidden message mentions another place you might go, but not as often and only when you play.

```
                    I
                 L  N  N
              I  A  M  O  E
           B  N  V  O  R  C  H
        R  F  P  A  O  O  L  L  C
     A  I  R  E  T  E  F  A  C  Y  T
  R  T  H  I  S  O  G  E  S  O  P  P  I
Y    B  Y  E  N  R  A  L  S  L  A  Y       K
     A  R  N  P  Y  R  L  A  R  A  C
     S  E  D  D  R  A  Y  K  C  A  B
     E  C  S  E  T  G  O  G  T  O  U
     M  O  H  I  R  S  P  E  A  S  S
     E  R  O  O  U  T  S  I  D  E  S
     N  G  U  R  O  O  K  E  P  I  T
     T  N  S  L  L  A  M  M  V  O
     D  A  E  C  E  N  I  L  N  O  P
     C  E  Y  O  U  R  R  O  O  M  H
```

BACKYARD	GARAGE	ON-LINE
BASEMENT	GROCERY	OUTSIDE
BUS STOP	HOME	PARK
CAFETERIA	KITCHEN	PLAYGROUND
CLASS	LAVATORY	SCHOOL
CLOSET	LIBRARY	STORE
FRIEND'S HOUSE	MALL	YOUR ROOM
	MOVIES	

33. SIX OF ONE

Shaped like a six-sided cube, the grid contains 26 six-letter words. But one letter is missing from the middle of each word in the word list. Before you circle words in the grid, fill in each blank in the word list with a different letter of the alphabet. Each letter will be used exactly once, so you can cross off each letter in the alphabet given as you go along. After you've found all 26 words in the grid, the hidden message will yield a ten-word sentence in which each word is exactly six letters long. If you need help, the complete word list can be found on page 65.

```
            T  W  E  L  T  A  B  M  O  C
         L  E  U  Q  E  S  V  O  E  H  U
      N  S  G  U  P  R  S  T  U  D  I  O
   F  A  M  O  U  S  I  H  Y  P  S  A  P
E  E  E  T  D  Y  Z  E  C  A  L  M  E  R
E  L  E     V     R        K  A  B  E  R
P  A  S  S  C  Z  A  O  O     Z  L  W  M  T
E  E  P  Y  R  U  J  N  I  E  D  S  E  A  C
I  N  Y  R  A  O  S  S  D     N  A  G  R  A
T  O  I  D  Y  B  O  X  C  A  R  F  S  S  L
H  S  N  G  O  C  Y  P  L     L  E  A  U
E  I  G  I  N  C  F  O  R  E  S  T  F
R  E  N  O  S  E  K  E  A     T  Y
I  R  R  N  G  P  L  E  A  N  O
T  B  S  N  E  V  I  R  D  J
```

A B C D E F G H I J K L M N O P Q R S T U V W X Y Z

1. AMA_ED	10. EIT_ER	18. PIC_LE
2. ANS_ER	11. EN_INE	19. PLE_SE
3. BO_CAR	12. FA_OUS	20. QU_TES
4. BRO_CO	13. FO_EST	21. SAF_TY
5. CA_MER	14. IN_URY	22. SE_UEL
6. COM_AT	15. JOY_UL	23. SPY_NG
7. CRA_ON	16. MO_HER	24. ST_DIO
8. DO_KED	17. NO_IER	25. TEM_TS
9. DRI_EN		26. VAN_AL

34. SHAKE ON IT

Shaped like a snow globe, the grid contains things you shake. The hidden message is a punny warning relating to the shape.

```
          H  O  L  D  L
       E  E  R  T  E  L  P  P  A
    T  F  I  G  D  E  P  P  A  R  W
 I  N  G  S  A  B  S  N  D  O  L  W  B
 G  L  T  A  M  B  O  U  R  I  N  E  O
 O  B  E  L  C  A  H  B  A  N  C  M  G
 A  H  C  T  E  K  S  A  H  C  T  E  G
 A  F  I  S  T  A  T  B  N  K  O  E  L
 D  A  E  H  R  U  O  Y  Y  D  O  L  E
 M  A  R  A  C  A  S  B  U  F  S  E  D
    E  L  K  R  S  M  O  P  M  O  P
       E  E  R  A  T  T  L  E  A
          R  L  L  Y  T  S  L
       H  S  N  O  W  G  L  O  B  E  A
    K  N  O  T  R  A  C  E  C  I  U  J  Y
```

A COLD	JELL-O
A FIST AT	JUICE CARTON
A LEG	MARACAS
APPLE TREE	POMPOMS
BABY BOTTLE	RATTLE
BELL	SALT SHAKER
BOGGLE	SNOW GLOBE
DICE	TAMBOURINE
ETCH-A-SKETCH	WRAPPED GIFT
HANDS	YOUR HEAD

35. THAT'S STRETCHING IT

Shaped like a Slinky toy walking down stairs, the grid contains things you stretch or that stretch. The hidden message answers the riddle "What would a contortionist say is his favorite part of a baseball game?"

```
        S Y K I T B S S
      N F K C T U H G E B
    A F D N A B R E B B U R
  K A S W I B A L L O O N G
E T S I L L Y P U T T Y G N E
L V N E E S     N T I E I A
A G H G A       E G E R C
S D U V I       N O C T C
T M N N N       I Y O S O
I A I I N       L G R W R
C S T R M       T E D O D
                S R P B I
                A E U T O
                O C H T N
                C E S O H
```

ACCORDION	LYCRA
[YOUR] BACK	[YOUR] MIND
BALLOON	ROPE
BOWSTRING	RUBBER BAND
BUBBLE GUM	SILLY PUTTY
BUNGEE CORD	SLINKY
CANVAS	SNAKE
COASTLINE	TAFFY
ELASTIC	[THE] TRUTH
HOSE	WINGS
[YOUR] LEGS	YOGI

36. MISSION TO MARS

Shaped like the planet Mars, the grid contains words and phrases associated with exploring that planet. The hidden message is a riddle and its answer about a manned mission to Mars.

```
            W  P  R  O  B  E
         H  D  A           A  F  T
      K  I  U  N           R  D  I  O
      R  G  U  S  E  V  C  R  A  T  E  R  L  S
      B  E  F  T  E  D  C  O  A  H  N  D  P  H
   Y  O  W  D  I  X  N  L  V  L  S  W  A  T  E  R
   A  U  S  T  P  P  A  R  E  A  N  C  O  N  M  A
   G  L  O  B  A  L  S  U  R  V  E  Y  O  R  A  U
   T  D  M  P  S  O  A  E  S  M  I  E  A  T  T  H
   W  E  H  A  E  R  M  N  I  N  G  T  S  W  I  H
   E  R  Y  C  R  A  S  S  E  U  H  O  O  L  T  D
      S  G  E  C  T  S  K  L  T  B  M  L  E  E
      T  O  C  H  I  I  L  C  O  O  S  E  I  R
         E  I  O  O  Y  A  H  O  R  M  M  A
         N  L  N  R  P  N  S  R  O  B
            A  R  S  S  S  S
```

BOULDERS	GUSEV CRATER	RED PLANET
CAMERAS	HEMATITE	ROCKS
DEIMOS	HILLS	ROVERS
DUST	ICE CAP	SAND
EARTH'S NEIGHBOR	LIFE?	SOIL
EXPLORATION	MARTIANS?	SPACE MISSION
GLOBAL SURVEYOR	PHOBOS	TWO MOONS
GULLY	PROBE	WATER

37. JUST SAY NO

Every item in the word list contains the letters NO in consecutive order. When these letters appear in the grid, each NO has been replaced by a "Halt!" sign [🚫] meaning "No!" Be sure to TAKE 🚫TE that the grid's shape resembles a road sign with a slash mark, which indicates not to do something, like No U-Turn. But do turn to the hidden message, which you'll 🚫TICE is a simple geographical fact.

```
            G M 🚫 E V E
          🚫 B O D Y S H O M E E
        I K 🚫 W 🚫 T H I N G 🚫 🚫 E
      🚫 A P I               K E G K
      E O O H S             🚫 🚫 R
    🚫 L I S B E 🚫           B A T
    Y Z H   R 🚫 🚫 🚫         E S C
    🚫 Z C     A X M N         L H Y
    X 🚫 C       L I E S       P A S
    R 🚫 🚫         U O N E       R 🚫 I
    Y T I         C U A N     I H 🚫
      P P U           🚫 S L S Z D
      O O F Q           I A 🚫 E R
        W 🚫 V E M B E R C B R A
          Y S T H A T S A 🚫 🚫
            C A N 🚫 N S
```

BINOCULARS	MONOPOLY	NOZZLE
CANNONS	NOAH'S ARK	OBNOXIOUS
CANOE	NOBEL PRIZE	PHENOMENAL
CASINOS	"NOBODY'S HOME!"	PINOCCHIO
EQUINOX	NOISY	SNOOPY
GNOME	NO-NONSENSE	SNORED
"I KNOW NOTHING!"	NOUNS	"THAT'S A NO-NO!"
KNOBS	NOVEMBER	VENOM

38. TAKING IT ALL IN

Shaped like a money bag, the grid contains things you take. The hidden message answers the riddle "Most people like to take, but what's something lots of people don't like to take?"

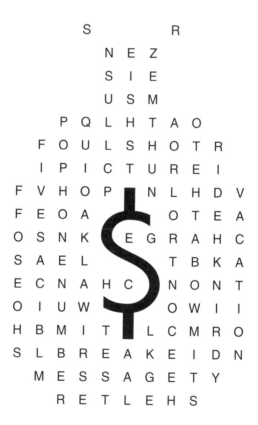

```
            S           R
          N  E  Z
          S  I  E
          U  S  M
       P  Q  L  H  T  A  O
    F  O  U  L  S  H  O  T  R
    I  P  I  C  T  U  R  E  I
 F  V  H  O  P     N  L  H  D  V
 F  E  O  A           O  T  E  A
 O  S  N  K     E  G  R  A  H  C
 S  A  E  L           T  B  K  A
 E  C  N  A  H  C     N  O  N  T
 O  I  U  W           O  W  I  I
 H  B  M  I  T        L  C  M  R  O
 S  L  B  R  E  A  K  E  I  D  N
    M  E  S  S  A  G  E  T  Y
    R  E  T  L  E  H  S
```

A BOW	FIVE	[A] RIDE
A NAP	[A] FOUL SHOT	SHELTER
[A] BATH	[A] LOOK	[YOUR] SHOES OFF
[A] BREAK	[A] MESSAGE	[A] TEST
[A] CHANCE	[AN] OATH	[YOUR] TIME
CHARGE	[A] PHONE NUMBER	[A] VACATION
CONTROL	[A] PICTURE	VITAMINS
[A] DRINK	[YOUR] PULSE	[A] WALK
	[A] QUIZ	

39. HOLD ON!

Shaped like a cell phone, the grid contains things you hold. The hidden message answers the riddle "What did the Olympic weight lifter say weighs absolutely nothing but is the hardest thing to hold?"

```
                        P
                        O
                        L
      A  H  T  A  E  R  B  I  N
      N  S  T  I  L  L  E  T  O
      E  U  G  N  O  T  W  I  I
      R  R              C  T
      I  B              A  A
      F  H              L  S
      G  T  W  B  O  G  K  O  R
      L  O  M  H  R  R  P  F  E
      I  O  L  U  O  I  R  F  V
      C  T  D  F  N  R  R  I  N
      N  G  N  I  C  E  S  C  O
      E  N  O  H  P  L  L  E  C
      P  N  S  M  L  L  U  D  S
      R  E  E  C  O  B  A  Y
      O  T  S  D  N  A  H  R  D
```

BABY	HANDS
[YOUR] BREATH	[YOUR] HORSES
CELL PHONE	[YOUR] NOSE
COMB	OPINION
CONVERSATION	PENCIL
DOLL	POLITICAL OFFICE
[YOUR] FIRE	STILL
FORK	[YOUR] TEMPER
GOLF CLUB	[YOUR] TONGUE
GRUDGE	TOOTHBRUSH

49

40. WATERLOGGED

Shaped like a drop of water, the grid contains words and phrases that all contain at least two H's and one O or H₂O, the chemical symbol for water. The hidden message is a sentence that contains three more "water"-filled words.

```
                    D
                    I
                P   S   T
                O   H   I
            T   O   C   A   H
        O   U   M   L   U   R   G
        G   G   P   O   H   H   A
    H   H   H   A   T   T   I   O
  E   S   U   O   H   H   G   U   O   R   H
  S   U   L   U   P   S   A   O   W   K   O
H   W   R   A   L   A   A   O   M   O   P   L   H
E   I   B   H   I   H   G   U   O   C   C   I   H
A   T   H   O   S   O   T   H   T   H   O   H   G
V   H   T   O   H   R   H   A   D   H   W   S   R
E   H   O   P   P   S   H   O   N   I   F   U   A
H   O   O   C   I   L   O   H   A   P   O   H   S
O   L   T   F   R   E   N   C   H   H   O   R   N
    D   T   W   H   I   T   E   H   O   T   H
        H   O   G   W   A   S   H   P   O
            R   N   M   U   H   O   H
                B   R   U   S   H
```

DISHCLOTH	HIP-HOP	RUSH HOUR
FISHHOOK	HOGWASH	SHILOH
FRENCH HORN	HO-HUM	SHOPAHOLIC
GHOULISH	HULA HOOP	THOUGH
HAND-TO-MOUTH	OOMPAH-PAH	TOOTHBRUSH
HEAVE-HO	PHARAOH	WHITE-HOT
HICCOUGH	ROUGHHOUSE	WHOOSH
HI-HO		WITHHOLD

41. PAY ATTENTION!

Shaped like a stop sign, the grid contains words and phrases that are often followed by an exclamation point. The hidden message is one more such exclamation, which appropriately comes at the very end.

```
          W  A  I  T  I
       E  A  C  C  M  N  D
    H  A  M  E  M  G  E  Y  A
    P  R  O  J  E  E  N  V  O  N  R
 O  G  O  B  L  T  S  O  E  U  K  T  N
 H  G  O  T  O  Y  O  U  R  R  O  O  M
 N  I  I  U  S  L  L  H  A  E  W  O  W
 O  N  T  K  D  I  C  H  E  A  O  H  W
 G  M  N  O  U  S  S  C  Y  L  K  S  S
    T  I  H  C  T  A  W  N  I  P  T
       I  G  K  E  W  U  T  A  A
       W  O  N  T  O  N  R
          O  S  A  F  F
                H
                T
                E
                I
                U
                Q
                E
                B
```

AARGH!	LISTEN!	RATS!
BE QUIET!	NEVER!	SHARK!
DARN!	NOT NOW!	SHOOT!
DUCK!	NO WAY!	STOP!
GET OUT!	NUTS!	THAT WAS CLOSE!
GO TO YOUR ROOM!	OH, NO!	WAIT!
HELP!	OMIGOSH!	WATCH IT!
I'M MELTING!	PHEW!	WHOA!
I OBJECT!		YOU'RE A LIAR!

51

42. KNOCK IT OFF!

Shaped like stacked bottles in a carnival game, the grid contains games and other things associated with a carnival. The hidden message answers the riddle "What was the restless boy doing when he played ring toss while riding the merry-go-round?"

```
            T  S  O
               S
               S  O  S
         P  I  T  C  H
         C  D  G  I  H
         A  N  N  S  H
         R  I  I  O  T
         N  F  R  I  P
         Y  S  P  R  G
         E  T  A  S  I
   N  D  R  H        L  F  L  T
      A  E           W  L
   C  C  G  S        U  B  O  E
E  A  B  N  N  D   R  T  A  D  B  N
T  R  O  I  A  U   R  O  L  E  I  S
R  O  T  R  C  C   I  Y  L  I  P  W
I  U  T  L  K  K   D  G  O  P  R  O
U  S  L  L  L  S   E  U  O  W  I  R
Q  E  E  E  I  N   S  N  N  E  Z  H
S  L  S  B  M  G   B  U  C  K  E  T
```

AIR RIFLE	DARTS	POND
BALLOON	DUCKS	PRIZE
BELL-RINGER	DUNK	RIDES
BOTTLES	FISH	RING TOSS
BOWLS	HORSE RACE	SQUIRT
BUCKET	KEWPIE DOLL	THROWS
CARNY	MILK CANS	TIP THE CAT
CAROUSEL	PITCH	TOY GUN

43. WHAT SMELLS?

Shaped like a flower, the grid contains things that have distinctive odors. The hidden message offers three more things that definitely fit this description.

```
                    T
          F         N           I
    E         S     I     S           H
       G    F  U  M  E  S     P
          N  M  I  A  A  R  O
          K  E  A  A  N  T  P  F
    R  E  C  I  R  O  C  I  L  E  S
          R  A  H  O  L  E  A
          B  U  R  P  N  D  N
       R     N  O  M  E  L     S
    Y        A     A     N           E
          D        H        B
E                  S                    N
    M  S           K           C  O
    A  U  E        U           I  C  D
       B  F  W     N     G  A  R
          Y  R  E  K  A  B  E
          A  E  R  T  H
                P
```

BACON	MINT
BAKERY	ORANGE
BARN	PERFUME
CIGAR	POPCORN
FUMES	SEA AIR
INCENSE	SEWER
LEMON	SHAMPOO
LICORICE	SKUNK

44. TAKIN' THE RAP

Shaped somewhat like a famous cartoon character, the grid contains rhyming words that complete each line in the "rap song" on the opposite page. But it's up to you to figure out what those rhymes are. The lines are in couplets, so lines 1 and 2 rhyme, lines 3 and 4 rhyme, and so on. As a hint, the blanks at the end of each line tell you the number of letters in each missing word. If you get stuck, look for words in the grid that might fit the rhymes. After you've circled all the rhyming words in the grid, read the hidden message to learn an interesting fact about the famous character, who is mentioned at the beginning and end of the rap song. If you need help, the complete word list on page 66.

RAP SONG

My name is Walt, like Mickey's maker _ _ _ _ _ _ ,
And for fun I like to toss around a _ _ _ _ _ _ _ .

It just spins so nicely till it lands upon the _ _ _ _ _ _ ,
Where it stops so quietly and barely makes a _ _ _ _ _ .

And I also like to snowboard up on top of the _ _ _ _ _ _ _ _ .
I go down so often I lose track of my _ _ _ _ _ _ _ ' .

It's a rush to feel the wind blowin' through my _ _ _ _ ,
And I'll do the hardest trails, but only on a _ _ _ _ .

In the summer, I go surfin' in the deep blue _ _ _ _ _
As I speed along on waves that provide me all the _ _ _ _ _ _ .

It's so great to hang ten while I hang out with my _ _ _ _ _ _ _ ,
Especially with school out, when we're done with all
    our _ _ _ _ _ _ _ .

But you've got to watch out for those great white _ _ _ _ _ _
'Cause their big, sharp teeth can leave some awfully
    nasty _ _ _ _ _ .

Just to think about it leaves me with a queasy _ _ _ _ _ _ _ .
The thought of getting chomped on I find
    very _ _ _ _ _ _ _ _ _ _ .

What sounds good is goin' home to eat a tasty _ _ _ _ _
Like cookies or Doritos or a box of _ _ _ _ _ _ _ _ _ _ _ .

Or maybe I'll have cheese as I kick back at my _ _ _ _ _ .
Ah, it's good to curl up and be quiet as a _ _ _ _ _ .

Which brings us back to Mickey and my flying
    disc _ _ _ _ _ _ _ _ .
I think I've said it all, so I really must be _ _ _ _ _ .

45. MARKING ON THE CURVE

Shaped like an arched doorway, the grid contains things that are always or often curved. The hidden message completes this riddle and answer: "Why did the dishonest athlete curl up the referee's rule book? Because he wanted ..."

```
          L  E  T  T  E  R  C
       A  N  A  N  A  B  I  T  H
    R  A  I  N  B  O  W  B  O  O  B
 N  E  S  T  L  O  U  I  S  A  R  C  H
 O  N  C  D  M        T  U  S  K  A
K O  S  U  E              T  E  F  W  H
R M  W  R                 S  I  K  E
O T  A  L                 H  S  S  E
F N  N  I                 O  H  B  M
G E  S  C                 E  H  E  O
N C  N  U                 R  O  A  D
I S  E  E                 R  O  K  R
N E  C  B                 S  K  I  S
U R  K  U                 S  N  E  L
T C  U  T                 G  L  E  S
```

BANANA	RAINBOW
BOOMERANG	RIBS
CRESCENT MOON	RING
CURLICUE	ROAD
DOME	SKIS
FISHHOOK	ST. LOUIS ARCH
HAWK'S BEAK	SWAN'S NECK
HORSESHOE	TUBE
LENS	TUNING FORK
[THE] LETTER C	TUSK

46. OPEN THE DOOR!

Shaped like a refrigerator, the grid contains things often found in a refrigerator. The hidden message answers the riddle "What's the easiest way to make good food?"

```
C  T  U  P  P  E  R  W  A  R  E
P  H  A  N  S  M  I  L  K  G  S
U  E  M  Y  A  R  T  G  G  E  I
S  S  H  E  L  V  E  S  T  C  A
T     R     A     H     E     N
A  C  B  E  D  T  M  C  C  F  N
C  S  A  I  D  R  U  R  I  S  O
R  R  K  T  R  B  S  E  U     Y
I  E  I  L  E  E  T  T  J     A
S  V  N  S  S  T  A  T  E     M
P  O  G  N  S  T  R  U  G  O  Y
E  T  S  T  I  E  D  B  N  R  L
R  F  O  I  N  D  N  G  A  O  L
O  E  D  D  G  T  V  O  R  A  E
N  L  A  T  O  M  A  T  O  F  J
```

BAKING SODA	MEAT
BUTTER	MILK
CATSUP	MUSTARD
CREAM	ORANGE JUICE
CRISPER	SALAD DRESSING
EGG TRAY	SHELVES
ICE CUBES	TOMATO
JELLY	TUPPERWARE
LEFTOVERS	TV DINNER
MAYONNAISE	YOGURT

47. SEA HERE!

Every item in the word list contains the letters SEA in consecutive order. When these letters appear in the sea-horse-shaped grid, they have been replaced by a 🌊 (sea wave). So, for example, the phrase ARRIVES EARLY in the list would appear as ARRIVE🌊RLY in the grid. The hidden message completes this statement: "For gamblers in a movie about a famous racehorse, it was hard to ..."

```
              🌊  I  L  🌊
           O  N  B  N  🌊  D  B
        T  🌊  K  C  A  B  E  E
        M  🌊  E     🌊  S  H  O  R  E
        T  T  T        O  S
        N  B  D  E
  🌊        E  🌊  N  L
     N  B  L  I  I  E
     🌊  P  T  T  H  V
     B  🌊  E  E  S  E
     S  I  P  N  D  L
  Y        U  C  N  🌊
     🌊  G  E  🌊  S
     W  N  N  I
     E  I  T  R        C  E
     E  L  🌊  U     I     L
     D  🌊  C  C           T
        T  H  🌊  R  C  H  T
        L  I  V  E  D  🌊
```

BACK SEAT	SEABED	SEARCH
INSEAM	SEA DEVIL	SEASHORE
"IT'S EASY!"	SEA LEVEL	SEAT BELT
"LET'S EAT!"	SEALING UP	SEATTLE
RED SEA	SEANCE	SEAWEED
RISE AND SHINE	SEAN PENN	TEN CENTS EACH
SEA BASS		WISEACRE

48. ZIP IT UP

Shaped like zipper latch and part of a zipper, the grid contains things that often have a zipper. The hidden message poses the question "If you have to dress right to follow a dress code, do you have to …"

```
 S                                       J
   T                                   A
     O                             C
       O           L           K
       G  A  B  G  N  I  P  E  E  L  S
       Z  I  N  Y  P  N  R  T  D  I  T
       L  G  W  M     I     H  R  N  T
          U  O  B     N     T  E  O
          F  G  A     G     T  S  O
             L  G           L  S
                O  A  W  A  K
                T  Z  G  I  E
                K  O  R  E  Y
                C  T  T  I  C
                A  P  C  E  A
                P  A  N  T  S
                K           E
                C           S
                A           R
                B  O  D  E  U
                A  K  R  A  P
```

BACKPACK	LUGGAGE
BOOTS	PANTS
DRESS	PARKA
GOWN	PURSES
GYM BAG	SKIRT
JACKET	SLEEPING BAG
KEY CASE	TENT
LINING	TOTES

49. GET IT WHITE

Shaped like a castle in chess (a game in which half the pieces are white), the grid contains things that are always or often white. The hidden message answers the riddle "What did Santa say when he disagreed with the weather forecast for no snow on Christmas?"

```
P  I     E  T  W     Y  S
G  E  N  O  C  H  L  N  N
A  T  A  L  L  I  N  A  V
      W  R  L  T  R
      S  U  L  E  R
      K  L  A  H  C
      N  O  K  O  U
      C  L  O  U  D
      I  O  N  S  T
   M  N  I  T  E  S  T
   N  C  O  E  T  N  A
   O  L  T  I  L  O  I
R  I  H  W  H  S  W  N  L
N  U  N  D  E  R  W  E  A  R  I
T  P  O  L  A  R  B  E  A  R  E
```

CHALK	POLAR BEAR
CLOUD	RICE
COTTON	SNOW
LILY	SWAN
LINEN	TEETH
MILK	UNDERWEAR
NOISE	UNICORN
ONION	VANILLA [ICE CREAM]
PEARL	[THE] WHITE HOUSE

50. A THIRST FOR WORDS

Shaped like a drinking glass, the grid contains beverages kids like to drink. The hidden message is a punny statement about a certain kind of athlete.

```
A  B  S  O  W  E  V  I  A  N  X
L  E  M  O  N  A  D  E  E  R  G
S  A  O  C  O  C  T  O  H  O  F
A  V  O  O  R  D  A  E  N  I  T
R  A  T  C  E  N  N  G  R  S  E
   D  H  C  R  R  G  I  O  N
   K  I  I  S  E  R  D  P  I
      E  L  P  P  A  N  S
         U  U  P  P  P
         N  E  E
         E  P  J
         V  R  U
         E  D  I
         S  N  C
         C  O  E
   M  I  L  K  S  H  A  K  E
   R  E  E  B  T  O  O  R  H
```

COKE	NECTAR
DR PEPPER	PEPSI
EGGNOG	ROOT BEER
EVIAN	SEVEN-UP
GRAPE JUICE	SMOOTHIE
HOT COCOA	SNAPPLE
ICED TEA	SODA
LEMONADE	TANG
MILK SHAKE	WATER

51. Y NOT?

The Y-shaped grid contains things starting with the letter Y. The hidden message is a famous Y-word from the world of cartoons.

```
N  Y  Y                              Y  A  A
W  B  S  A                        A  Y  B  G
A  Y  E  A  H                  R  A  E  N  O
Y  U  K  O  N  O            D  L  E  I  Y  Y
   A  I  T  E  Y  O      S  E  Z  M  D  Y
      Y  E  L  L  O  W  S  T  O  N  E
         O  A  Y  Y  B  H  A  T  S
            L  A  O  A  Y  S  T
               K  Y  L  A  E
               K  B  E  R  E
               E  Y  D  M  K
               T  A  O  U  N
               Y  A  Y  L  A
               Y  U  C  K  Y
               A  M  M  E  D
               K  O  C  M  O
               T  H  C  A  Y
```

YACHT	YARMULKE	YMCA
YAHOO	YAWN	YODEL
YAHTZEE	YEAH	YOGA
YAKKETY-YAK	YEAST	YOLK
YALE	YELLOWSTONE	YO-YO
YANKEES	YESTERDAY	YUCKY
YAO MING	YETI	YUKON
YARDS	YIELD	YUMMY
	"YIKES!"	

52. MARDI GRAS

Shaped like a mask, the grid contains things associated with Mardi Gras. New Orleans is the U.S. city most famous for celebrating Mardi Gras. Krewes are social organizations that sponsor parade floats, masked balls and other activities. Krewe names often come from mythology, such as Argus, Bacchus, and Saturn. (Zulu is a Krewe that was formed to spoof other Krewes.) Costumed riders on floats toss "throws" to parade watchers. These throws are trinkets such as beads, drinking cups, and two other items found in the hidden message.

```
S                             B
E  Z                       M  A
M  E  U  D              S  P  U  C
U  F  L  L  A  B  D  E  K  S  A  M  C
T  A  A  L  U  T  K  C  T  L  I  K  H
S  T        R  H  A           I  U
O  T  O  N  E  W  O  R  L  E  A  N  S
C  U  E  W  R  L  N  N  O  N  E  G  C
K  E  E  K  F  U  L  I  A  W  T  C  C
   S  E  C  N  S  T  V  A  N  S  A
   D     N  I  N  A  E        K
   A  D     D  A  R  L  S     O  E
   Y  R     U  D  T        D  S
      T  G              A  B
      L  R  U           R  O  O
         N  A  S  D  A  E  B
            P  P  S
```

ARGUS	FAT TUESDAY	NEW ORLEANS
BACCHUS	FLOATS	PARADE
BEADS	KING CAKES	PARTY
CARNIVAL	KREWES	SATURN
COSTUMES	LENT	"THROWS"
CUPS	MASKED BALL	TRINKETS
DANCE		ZULU

53. ONE LAST TIME

Every item in the word list contains the letters TIME in consecutive order. When these letters appear in the grid, they have been replaced by a ⏰. So, for example, the phrase TIME MACHINE in the list would appear as ⏰MACHINE in the grid. So TAKE YOUR ⏰ and HAVE THE ⏰ OF YOUR LIFE. Both the hidden message and the grid, which is shaped like an alarm clock set at a quarter to 12, are ⏰LY reminders that we're rapidly reaching our ⏰ LIMIT.

AIRTIME	MARK TIME	TIME AND TIME AGAIN
ANYTIME	MULTIMEDIA	TIME LAG
AT TIMES	NAP TIME	TIMELESS
BEDTIME	PASTIME	TIMELINE
BIG TIME	PRIME TIME	TIME-OUT
DAYTIME	SCHOOLTIME	TIMES SIGN
DOWNTIME	SENTIMENTS	"TIME'S UP!"
IN NO TIME	SOMETIME	TIME ZONE
"IT'S TIME!"	SPRINGTIME	"WHAT TIME IS IT?"

12. TAKE NOTE WORD LIST

1. APPLE
2. BATS
3. BLUE
4. BOWS
5. CASTLE
6. CHEST
7. CUBS
8. DIAMOND
9. DRESSES
10. EAGLE
11. IRON
12. LEAVES
13. MATCH
14. NOTES
15. PAGE
16. RACKET
17. ROSE
18. STAR
19. TAPES

23. BEFORE AND AFTER WORD LIST

1. BILL
2. BLIND
3. CHOCOLATE
4. CIRCLE
5. DIAMOND
6. EVERYBODY
7. FAIRY
8. FOOTBALL
9. FOUNTAIN
10. HOCKEY
11. HOOP
12. INDEPENDENCE
13. LIBRARY
14. MAGIC
15. PARTY
16. SCHOOL
17. TABLE
18. TEST
19. WASHINGTON
20. WEATHER

33. SIX OF ONE WORD LIST

1. AMAZED
2. ANSWER
3. BOXCAR
4. BRONCO
5. CALMER
6. COMBAT
7. CRAYON
8. DOCKED
9. DRIVEN
10. EITHER
11. ENGINE
12. FAMOUS
13. FOREST
14. INJURY
15. JOYFUL
16. MOTHER
17. NOSIER
18. PICKLE
19. PLEASE
20. QUOTES
21. SAFETY
22. SEQUEL
23. SPYING
24. STUDIO
25. TEMPTS
26. VANDAL

44. TAKIN' THE RAP WORD LIST

In order by rhyme:

DISNEY
FRISBEE

GROUND
SOUND

MOUNTAIN
COUNTIN'

HAIR
DARE

OCEAN
MOTION

BUDDIES
STUDIES

SHARKS
MARKS

FEELING
UNAPPEALING

SNACK
CRACKER JACK

HOUSE
MOUSE

THROWING
GOING

1. THAT'S FANTASTIC!

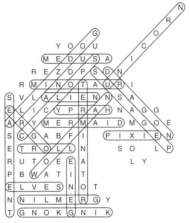

"You're driving me absolutely batty!"

2. BE A GOOD SPORT

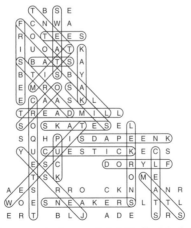

Because she's a rock 'n' Rollerblader.

3. WHIRLED VIEW

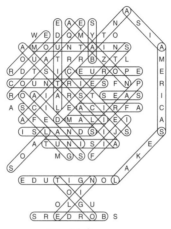

World-famous.

4. UP A TREE

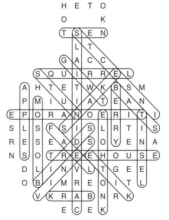

He took chemis-tree and geome-tree.

5. 2, 4, 6, 8

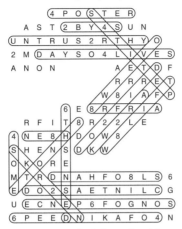

A stunt<u>wo</u>man on a fr<u>eigh</u>ter fired her <u>six</u>-gun.

6. POOL PARTY

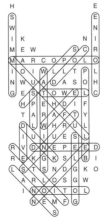

He knew it was either sink or swim.

7. CAN YOU STAND IT?

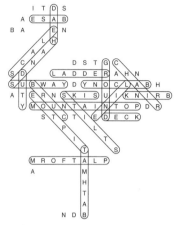

It's a bandstand handstand.

8. MY I

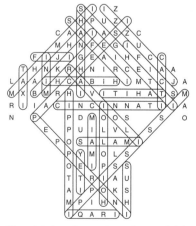

Zucchini, calamari, and souvlaki.

9. BLOWHARDS

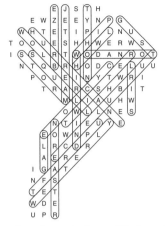

She went into her windup with the wind up.

10. TEAM PLAYERS

Bengal, Colt, Falcon, Jaguar, Jet, Ram.

11. PLAY GROUND

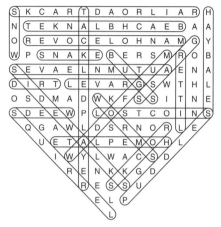

A person who's making a snow angel.

12. TAKE NOTE

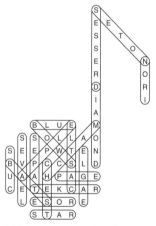

[See the hidden message in the next puzzle.]

13. THE SOUND OF MUSIC

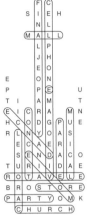

She put it in her "note"book.

14. WINGING IT

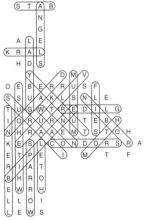

"... a horse that flies?"

15. IT'S ONLY MONEY

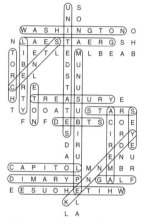

"Soon she'll be able to afford an umbrella."

16. IN A FIX

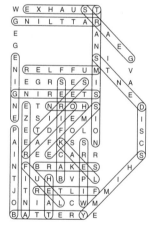

We give great self-service.

17. AW, CHUTE!

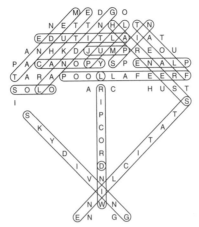

"... don't take up parachuting."

18. OFF WITH HER HEAD!

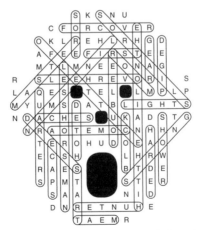

Knuckle, hammer, sleepy, and thunder.

19. JUMP FOR JOY

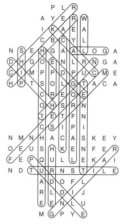

Playing a game can make you feel kind of jumpy.

20. A TALL TALE

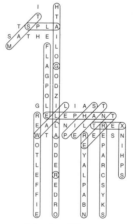

It's the Giants.

21. THAT'S NEWS TO ME!

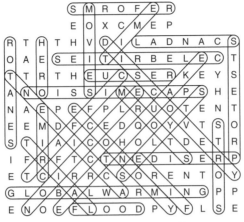

"... except that they happened to different people."

22. HOT STUFF

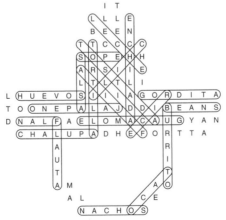

It'll be chili today and hot tamale.

23. BEFORE AND AFTER

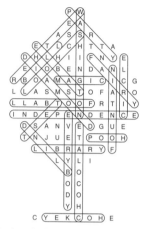

Stained glass of orange juice.

24. CLEAN UP YOUR ACT

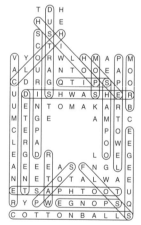

They wanted to make a clean getaway.

25. FOWL PLAY

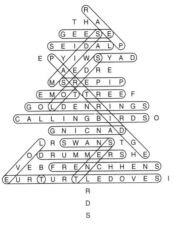

"... they were for the birds."

26. HOW SWEET IT IS

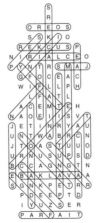

"... so now I have it as an appetizer."

27. TAKE A BREAK

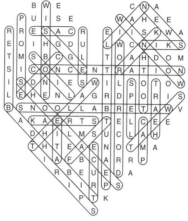

Because he said, "Come on. Give me a break!"

28. TOOLING ALONG

"... held up a hammer and saw."

29. HURRY UP AND GET DOWN TO BUSINESS

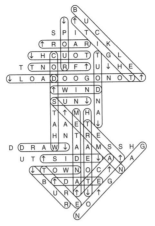

"Sit down and shut up!"

30. ROLL CALL

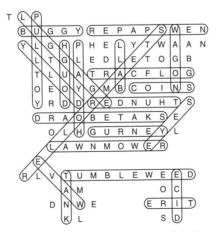

They wanted to be "roll models."

31. STRIP SEARCH

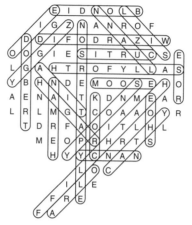

Garfield and Mallard Fillmore.
[James A. Garfield and Millard Fillmore]

32. GOING PLACES

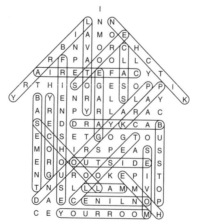

In Monopoly, the only "place" to go is Park Place.

33. SIX OF ONE

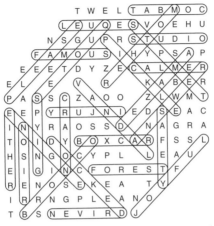

Twelve hungry, speedy zebras zoomed
across grassy plains eating plants.

34. SHAKE ON IT

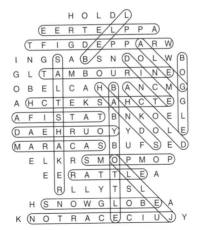

Holding a snow globe can make you feel really shaky.

35. THAT'S STRETCHING IT

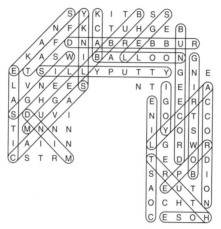

"It's the seventh-inning stretch."

36. MISSION TO MARS

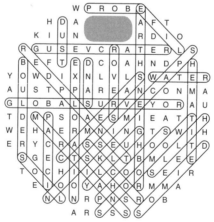

What kind of candy will astronauts eat when they get here?
Mars Bars.

37. JUST SAY NO

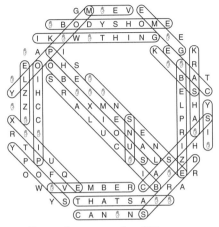

Genoa is <u>not</u> <u>n</u>orth of <u>No</u>rway.

38. TAKING IT ALL IN

Responsibility.

39. HOLD ON!

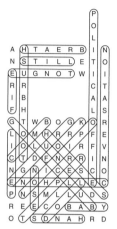

A new world record.

40. WATERLOGGED

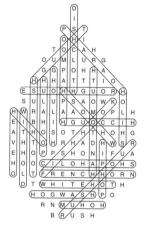

I thought I saw a photograph of a thornbush.

41. PAY ATTENTION!

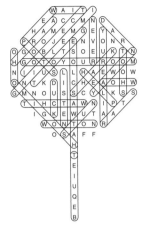

"C'mon now, knock it off!"

42. KNOCK IT OFF!

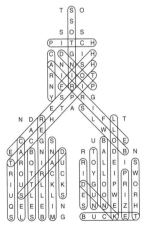

Tossing and turning.

43. WHAT SMELLS?

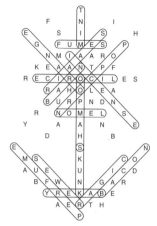

Fish market, fresh laundry, and bad breath.

44. TAKIN' THE RAP

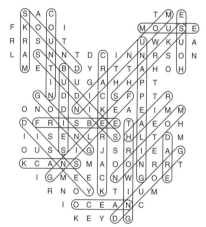

At first, Walt Disney thought to name his mouse Mortimer, not Mickey.

45. MARKING ON THE CURVE

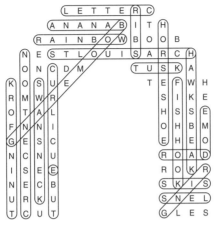

"... to bend the rules."

46. OPEN THE DOOR!

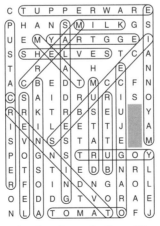

Change the first letter in "good" to an F.

47. SEA HERE!

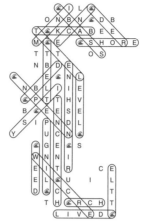

"... lose a bet on Seabiscuit."

48. ZIP IT UP

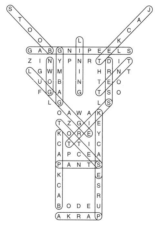

"... zip right to follow a Zip Code?"

49. GET IT WHITE

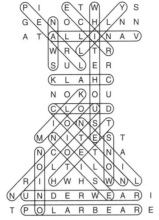

"It's gonna turn out all white."

50. A THIRST FOR WORDS

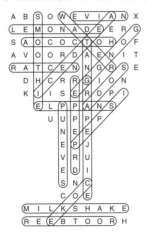

A boxer's favorite drink is punch.

51. Y NOT?

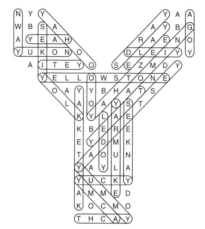

Yabba-dabba-doo!

52. MARDI GRAS

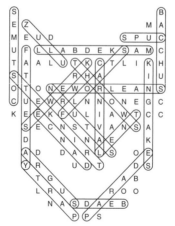

Medallion necklaces and doubloons.

53. ONE LAST TIME

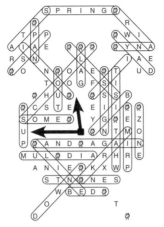

We're out of <u>time</u>. See ya next <u>time</u>.

Index
Italics indicate answer page number

• • •

About the Author

Mark Danna earns his living writing puzzles: more than 20 word search books; the newspaper-syndicated, rhymes-with-clues *Wordy Gurdy*; American Mensa's annual page-a-day calendar *365 Brain Puzzlers*; and some 200 crosswords, including Sundays in *The New York Times*. Danna has been an associate editor at *Games* magazine and a staff writer for *Who Wants to Be a Millionaire*. To order personalized word searches, crosswords, or other puzzles, contact Mark at puzzlestogo@gmail.com.

Also by Mark Danna

Amazing Word Search Puzzles for Kids
Brain Aerobics: Word Search Puzzles
Clever Word Search Puzzles for Kids
Great Word Search Puzzles for Kids
Large Print Word Search Puzzles
Large Print Word Search Puzzles 2
Petite Elegant Word Searches
Scattergories Word Search Puzzles
Word Search Puzzles to Keep You Sharp